Copyright © 2014, 2018 by J. N. Cook

All rights reserved under International and Pan-American Copyright Conventions. Published in the United States.

Kindle Direct Publishing

ISBN: 9781718073234

FOREWORD

Some years ago I was asked to draft what has become this booklet for my local parish's RCIA ministry. We had (and still have) a Spirited team of individuals who teach the faith to a dozen or so new catechumens each year. What we soon found lacking in our ministry was a short and simple, straight-forward document that would explain and answer questions *of the Mass* while the Mass was taking place, while the rest of us were in prayer.

The idea came from the suggestion that perhaps our catechumens should not attend Mass with the team until they are fully educated on it, as perhaps it would simply cause more confusion than good without first understanding it. Most of us disagreed, but understood the point. The compromise was this text—and it was greatly appreciated by the catechumens.

This booklet has since become an essential tool for those discerning the Rite of Christian Initiation in our parish. Now in print, I am convinced in Christ that you will benefit greatly from the information it contains, whether new to Catholicism, teaching the faith, simply curious or a long-time Catholic who simply never knew, *why are we doing this in the first place?*

- J. N. Cook

The Catholic Mass

*An Introduction for Those Discerning
the Rite of Christian Initiation for Adults*

By

J. N. Cook

INTRODUCTION

Due to its rich and extensive historical traditions, the Catholic Mass can be difficult to follow or understand for those new to the faith without proper overview. This difficulty too can be magnified by the fact that some of these traditions are still in flux today, and surely will continue, as humankind and Catholic understanding and teaching matures and develops over the millennia.

Yet, it is the central purpose, source and summit of what is practiced by Catholics, which has never deviated from the time of the apostles and earliest Christians: "that when we eat this bread and drink this cup, we proclaim [Jesus'] death and glory until [He] comes again" –the **Eucharist** (the *Blessed Sacrament*).

The traditional layout of the establishment in which to celebrate the Eucharist (the building) has both Traditional and Scriptural basis, though the Second Vatican Council came to agreement that deviating from a predefined, rigid architectural blueprint does not diminish the value or sanctity of the ceremony in any way, much less the Eucharist. [5] That said; the original structure was designed in theme of a ship or sailing

---

One notable disciplinary modification was in the early days of Christianity, as noted in Scripture [1] [2]: *sins were confessed publicly in front of the whole community. After years of awkwardness and withholding of sins, the Church modified the practice to be private and one on one with the priest.*

St. Luke recorded how the apostles taught the early Christians to "devote themselves to [their] teaching and the fellowship, to the breaking of bread and the prayers". [3]

The related verb to the Greek noun εὐχαριστία (eucharistia), meaning "thanksgiving," is found in the earliest account of the New Testament, as described by Eugene LaVerdiere (1996), "The Eucharist in the New Testament and the Early Church". [4]

vessel (specifically an ark), being that the parishioners were carried in their journey to Jesus. This is why the older buildings have all the pews facing the same direction, as on a ship. [6]

At the front of the older designed church buildings, in the direction the congregation faced, is the **Tabernacle** where the Eucharist resides. In front of the Tabernacle is the **Altar**. Both the Altar and the Tabernacle have ancient Hebrew origins. [7] Prior to Jesus' death, where He explained *He* is the **"Final Sacrifice"**, [8] the Hebrews had practiced the sacrifice of various animals in worship. But it was understood by the early Christians that by Jesus' teaching at the Last Supper, His death and resurrection, the sacrifice of any other life to God was to be concluded. Yet, the altar and tabernacle remain in the Catholic Church, as Jesus fulfilled the tradition with His own body.

The Catechism prior to the Second Vatican Council went into explicit detail as to why the church building must be built in the form of an ark, but such restrictions are not doctrinal and have been considerably relaxed. The comparison of Noah's salvation and Baptism is still reflected however: "The waters of the great flood you made a sign of the waters of Baptism, that make an end of sin and a new beginning of goodness." (CCC 1219) [9]

Tabernacle *(Hebrew:* משכן, *mishkan, "residence" or "dwelling place")*

Hebrews 10: 11-14, "And every priest stands daily ministering, and often offers the same sacrifices, which could never take away sins. But this man offering one sacrifice for sins, forever sits at the right hand of God, waiting until his enemies are made his footstool. For by one sacrifice he has forever perfected those who are saved." [10]

THE MASS

The **mission** or goal of the Catholic Mass is for the congregation to both individually and as a group come into *communion with Jesus Christ*. This mission is believed by Catholics to be successfully accomplished by several preparations, first and foremost prayer and examination of one's conscious.

UPON ENTERING THE CHURCH

The congregation enters and the people dip their fingers into water that has been blessed prior by a priest ("Holy Water"). They make the sign of the cross (touching their forehead, stating "in the name of the Father", touching their heart, stating "in the name of the Son" and making a cross left to right from shoulder to shoulder, stating "and in the name of the Holy Spirit", as a first-order spiritual cleansing, reminiscent of Baptism, a "sacramental". [9]

The notion of **Communion with Jesus** *comes from Jesus' teaching in the Bible "I in [the Father] and you in I",* [11] *which also comes from the biological science of our bodies becoming the very substance of that which we eat.*

The word "mass" comes from the late Latin term "missa", which literally means "dismissal", but in Christianity this term has come to be understood and translated as "mission". [12]

The first New Testament mention of a person having sins forgiven through another human being comes from John the Baptist, as Baptism involves forgiveness through the involvement of another human being (no one gets to baptize themselves). [13] *However, public/group forgiveness began at least 500 years prior.* [14] *This was all prior to Jesus' teaching of human to human forgiveness (reconciliation), as well as His teaching on God to human forgiveness through it. Thus, Catholics baptize children very young, so as to give even young children the opportunity to experience human to human forgiveness with divine intervention through holy reconciliation.* [9]

ENTERING THE PEW

The Catholic congregation selects any pew of their choosing, unless certain seating is assigned for them (such as with RCIA, weddings, etc.), but before they enter the pew, they are to direct their attention to the Tabernacle to genuflect on the right knee of recognition of the divine presence of Jesus as the Eucharist, of which resides in the Tabernacle. Additionally, any time one passes or walks in front of the Tabernacle, a Catholic is to bow or genuflect. [9] A lowering of one's head is acceptable, particularly when in precession (carrying the cross or Bible). [9]

What is most important to Catholic teaching is what's in one's heart out of respect for Jesus. [9] That said, genuflecting on the right knee is considered a sign of adoration, which is reserved for God. [9] Bowing or genuflecting on the left knee has been historically a show of respect (originally for kings or nobility), and therefore can be done before relics, the altar and similar. [9] One is supposed to genuflect whenever he or she passes before the Blessed Sacrament reposed within a

It was Alexander the Great who introduced the court-etiquette of bending on one knee before nobility in 328 BC. [15]

Later this etiquette was modified, such that when genuflecting before the divine king Jesus, Catholics use the right knee; for all other nobility the left knee is used. [9]

Bowing (or lowering of one's body) is a long held common practice throughout Asia and Europe. [16]

All altars today contain a saint's relic. [9] *This originated from the fact that the early Christians celebrated the Mass in secret, typically in tombs of the early Christian martyrs. When Christianity was legalized in the third and fourth centuries, the early Christians felt their altars were somehow empty without the remains of the martyrs.* [17]

The act of "examining one's conscience" prior to the Eucharist comes from St. Paul in his letters, describing the preparation of accepting the Eucharist.

In St. Paul's time some individuals from his various churches were coming to Mass simply to get something to eat and drink, often leaving nothing for the others, something that Paul taught was disgraceful. Thus, he urged that all should eat their fill prior to coming to Mass, and to examine their consciences prior to eating the Eucharist.

tabernacle (*General Instruction of the Roman Missal* 233). [18] And one is supposed to give a bow of his or her body whenever he or she passes in front of the altar (*Ceremonial of Bishops* 72). [19] When both the tabernacle and altar are present, or when walking between the altar and the tabernacle, one genuflects toward the Eucharist repose in the tabernacle. [9] Between Holy Thursday and the Easter Vigil (when the tabernacle is empty), a bow of one's body to the altar is the only option available. That said, adoration of the altar and the cross is permitted, [9] as they both represent Christ as a person, He being the final sacrifice itself and the cross and altar a part of that sacrifice. [9]

Upon entering the pew then, the congregation kneels in contemplative prayer before the Eucharist in the Tabernacle (before Jesus Himself...not the various statues, [9] nor the priest)—it is before the Eucharist, the sacrificed body as Catholics believe Jesus Himself willed in His teachings, and as St. Paul taught in his letters. [20] The prayer is typically an examination of one's conscience, also as St. Paul taught. [21] Often quiet, contemplative music is performed as the congregation prepares themselves for the Mass.

PRECESSIONAL

The priest and typically a deacon with a couple altar boys or girls precess toward the Tabernacle. Typically this is with music, and they most often precess from the back (though not necessarily [18]). The deacon carries the Bible, one altar boy or girl carries a crucifix and the other a candle, of which is a reminder of the presence of Jesus in the Mass. [18] Jesus' actual presence in the Mass follows Catholic belief in the Eucharist being His body and blood, but also from scriptural passage, as He explained, "where two or more are joined in my name, so too am I there." [22]

INTRODUCTORY RITES

The priest makes the sign of the cross, stating "**in the name of the Father, the Son and the Holy Spirit**", and the congregation responds "**Amen**" (meaning, "I acknowledge too

In modern times, Catholics are still taught to merely sip from the cup and the Body served remains a small piece of unleavened bread. However, as over-eating of the Eucharist has largely diminished in practice, the Catechism now teaches additional preparation by fasting one hour prior to taking communion. [9]

Fasting is a practice of many cultures, and was practiced also by Jesus and His apostles, [23] [24] *so as to cleanse one's body and spirit.*

Priests (often referred to as "presbyters" or in Greek "presbuteros" in the New Testament) were the elders who worked in the various churches with the Apostles (bishops) to be spiritual leaders and decision makers. [25] *But they also were consecrated to be the hands of Christ to His faithful. In Biblical times this consisted of healings, special blessings and the like.* [26] *These are all still practiced today in Catholicism, as taught to the early Christians by the apostles.*

Early historical priests were often married men, [27] but based on the spiritual recommendations of St. Paul ("it would be better to remain as I...to not marry" [28] because "a married man is attentive to his wife, while a single man attentive to God"[29]), and the Catholic Church has long held that a priest's family best remain the Church and their parishes, as a lifelong commitment. [9]

Deacons in the New Testament were anointed as servants to the Apostles (Bishops). [30] Today in Catholic practice they can give homilies (sermons), and thus are too teachers of the faith and leaders of prayer. They also have been ordained and consecrated to be the hands of Christ in certain sacraments as well. [9]

Men can become deacons if they are married or unmarried. However, once a deacon, it too is a lifelong commitment, and deacons understand that they will not be permitted to marry after ordination. [9]

A "sin" is considered a deliberate action, inaction or distraction not in line with our mission to God. [9] Catholicism acknowledges that we all sin, and therefore forgiveness to others is our gift...not judgment. [9]

that we are here in the name of the **Trinity**"). The priest gives a greeting in various forms signifying the presence of God, involving the blessing, "**may the Lord be with you**" and the congregation responds, "**and with your spirit**," greetings derived from the New Testament letters of St. Paul. [31]

PENITENTIAL ACT

The priest then invites the congregation to an act of penitence, a further preparation of the Eucharist, asking for the forgiveness of sins as taught in the Bible. [21] The first is the "Confiteor", which means "I confess". Then the priest offers a prayer of absolution of sins, which is similar (but lacking in efficacy [9]) to the Sacrament of Penance (the private individual acknowledgment and absolution of ones sins through a Priest, as forgiven by God). Both acts follow scripturally from Jesus' words, including those "whose sins you retain on Earth, so too will be retained in Heaven. And whose sins you forgive on earth, so too will be forgiven in Heaven". [32]

These acts are one sacramental example of the priest's unique anointing and ordination to be the hands of Jesus on Earth, as taught by Jesus to His apostles, who called for the laying on of hands (healing and forgiveness), who then continued it after He left. [26]

KYRIE AND GLORIA

What follows the priest's absolution is the congregation's own supplication for mercy: "Lord have Mercy. Christ have Mercy. Lord have Mercy." This is often a chant or song, which is followed by the "Gloria", the most ancient and venerable hymn of the Catholic Church. It is essentially the spiritually motivated praise and acknowledgement of God's glory in heaven, as maker of both heaven and earth, of all seen and unseen.

The Catholic Church has always held that all forgiveness comes from God alone. [9] *But it accepts Jesus' teaching that He has blessed us with the opportunity to have our sins forgiven on Earth from each other, similar to other gifts God has given us (healing of the sick, "moving mountains" if our faith is strong enough, etc.).* [33] *This would be comparable to the notion that all love comes from God alone, but we are also blessed to receive it and give it on Earth to each other as well. The belief holds that it is the Holy Spirit that "flows" through us to make such things possible.* [9]

The Second Vatican Council approved the Catholic Mass to be said in the vernacular languages throughout the world, [5] *though Latin still exists in some places and contexts.*

Latin words are common today in songs and prayers, particularly the Kyrie, which means "Lord" and Gloria, which means "Glory to…"

PRAYER

The priest then calls upon the congregation to pray. Often this involves a brief moment of contemplative silence. This prayer is to additionally prepare for communion with Jesus.

LITURGY OF THE WORD

With a few exceptions, two sections of the Bible are read by lay parishioners: a **First Reading** and a **Second Reading**. The First Reading is most often from the Old Testament and the Second Reading is most often from the New Testament teachings of the Apostles (Acts, letters from Paul, James, etc.). These readings are then followed by the **Gospel**, which is read by the deacon if one is present. The Gospel (meaning "good news" [37]) is specifically a teaching Jesus Himself gave in the New Testament. The selected readings and the Gospel are pre-determined for a specific date, following a three year cycle. [18] In other words, not the local priest, nor the bishop, nor even the pope in Rome, may personally choose what selections of the Bible are read at any given Mass. The benefit of this is

The word "liturgy" comes from the ancient Greek word "λειτουργι", which means work of the people. [34]

The New Testament speaks in numerous verses that Jesus was the "Word Made Flesh", [35] *and that a Spirit can be discerned to be Holy if it acknowledges that the Word Made Flesh is Lord.* [36] *Catholics believe too that the Bible itself is that same Word of God, in that study of the Bible is also the study of Jesus Himself...both Old and New Testaments.* [9]

that in that three year cycle, if an individual were to attend every mass given, then he or she would have heard from every book of the Bible in three years—more or less, not every word throughout however. [38]

Other benefits of this cycle is that readings and the Gospel can be read in advance if so desired, and that they are independent of unwarranted human influence of the times.

Following the readings, the priest or deacon gives his **homily** (similar to a sermon) on the readings and the Gospel. The Gospel and the two readings share commonality in theme, [18] and thus the Homily most often carries on this theme.

After the Homily, the congregation professes the **Nicene Creed**, which is typically found inside the cover of the hymnal. The Liturgy of the Word concludes with the Universal Prayer or Prayer of the Faithful, followed by intentions (supplications, prayers for peace in the world, prayers for the church, families of those who died or have just married, etc.).

If you just go to Mass on Sundays, you will hear 3.7% of the Old Testament and 40.8% of the New Testament. [38]

If you attend all Sunday and Weekday Masses, you will hear 13.5% of the Old Testament and 71.5% of the New Testament. [38]

Vatican II brought far more verses of the Bible into the Masses than in previous centuries. [5]

The word "homily" comes from the Greek word "ομιλειν", which means to have communion or hold verbal intercourse with a person.

This Nicene Creed (creed, meaning belief) is a statement and acknowledgment of the universal beliefs of the Catholic Church defined at Nicene. [39]

LITURGY OF THE EUCHARIST

"Transubstantiation", one of those words even many Catholics are not familiar with, is the notion that God has the ability (and holy interest) to transform a material, a thing or even the human body itself into something else, while its physical appearance remains intact. [9] The term is specifically regarded for the Eucharist, but the belief in this process is not dissimilar to Jesus being both God and man, or just about anything else He wants to become, while his appearance on Earth remained that of a human. It is believed from the events at the end of the New Testament Gospels (including the Last Supper), that He desired His human body to enter heaven intact, but chose a different form to still remain with us: that of "the Bread of Life".

Catholic charities feed, house and provide health and other human services to millions upon millions around the world and at home, has been referred to as the "World's Biggest Charity"—and has been at it for thousands of years. [40]

The tithing during Catholic masses also helps pay teachers' salaries so that Catholic spiritual education for children can remain part of the parish. [40]

The personal and individual preparations of communion have largely been established, and now the Mass moves more toward a **transubstantiated** preparation (preparation of the bread and wine to become the body and blood of Jesus).

While the bread and wine are delivered to the altar, most often carried by lay parishioners, the congregation is asked to remember the scriptural teaching of **tithing**, giving alms to the poor and to supporting the community. While each parish may have different manner of providing the congregation the means to be charitable (passing of a basket, basket in the back of church, etc.), Catholicism has long recognized that **charity** is not something that can be worked out of or over-looked in Christian faith, as charity is equated to love. [9] It is from Jesus' teachings on charity, first and foremost, that charity remains a part of the Catholic Mass (mission) today. [18]

Scripture expresses that all charitable love only comes from God, [41] and thus it must come from one's heart—coerced obligation could not equate to charity. [9] Instead, this act is an opportunity to let God's charitable love work through one's heart in preparation of communion with Jesus.

The wine and unleavened bread is carried to the altar, where the priest then recites quietly prayers and blessings of purification as he prepares the altar and the gifts.

The congregation has been seated at this point, but on the priests call, everyone stands.

The priest says aloud, "Pray, brethren, that my sacrifice and yours may be acceptable to God, the almighty Father." The congregation responds: "May the Lord accept the sacrifice at your hands, for the praise and glory of his name, for our good, and the good of all his holy Church." The priest then pronounces the variable prayer over the gifts that have been set aside.

Thereafter begins the Eucharistic Prayer, the most important part of the Mass. The priest then speaks to the congregation, "The Lord be with you", and the congregation responds "and with your spirit."

He continues, "Lift up your hearts."

The people respond with: "We lift them up to the Lord.

Unleavened bread contains no yeast, thus resisting spoilage, reminiscent of Hebrew journeys and feasts, and the Hebrew feast of unleavened bread. [42]

Catholics only use fine wheat for the Eucharist, based on scriptural passages and respect for the sacrament. [18]

Catholics only use fine wine from grapes, which cannot be without alcohol, as scripture teaches that at the wedding at Cana, Jesus turned water into the finest wine. [48] *Weak, much less non-alcoholic, would not have been considered fine wine in Jesus time.* [18]

While the priest adds a little water to the wine, it is reminiscent of Jesus's death and the Eucharistic rite, not about dilution of the alcohol. [18]

In the New Testament, Jesus lost many disciples on this teaching in his day, "how can we eat his body and drink his blood...this teaching is hard." [43]

The priest then says, "Let us give thanks to the Lord, our God."

The congregation agrees and says, "It is right and just." The priest then continues with one of many Eucharistic Prayer forewords, followed by the Sanctus acclamation, often in cantor (sung) by the priest. Much of this rite is often in cantor from the beginning, depending on the priest, parish or culture.

In the U.S., and some other countries, the congregation kneels right after the Sanctus acclamation.

The **Epiclesis** is then recited to implore the power of the Holy Spirit to the "gifts" that may become Christ's body and blood, and that this Communion may be salvation of the congregation who take part in it.

Then the priest in prayer recalls the words and actions of Jesus at the Last Supper and then includes expresses of offering and intercessions for the living and the dead.

The Liturgy of the Eucharist concludes with what is sometimes called the "great amen", signifying that the bread and wine are now accepted by the congregation as the body and blood of Jesus.

In 1 Corinthians 10, St. Paul writes, "I speak to you as wise men: judge ye yourselves what I say. [16] The chalice of benediction, which we bless, is it not the communion of the blood of Christ? And the bread, which we break, is it not the partaking of the body of the Lord? [17] For we, being many, are one bread, one body, all that partake of one bread." [20]

Epiclesis; from Ancient Greek, meaning "invocation" or "calling down from on high". [44]

While it may be impossible to fully understand Jesus' teaching of the Eucharist in human and earthly terms, the Catholic Church has held since its origins that this is not merely a parable or simile, [9] *as He never stated "this is like my body" or "this is like my blood", as He had with other teachings. He simply stated it as is, and Catholics today accept it as such.*

COMMUNION RITE

Jesus gave but one prayer to his disciples, and this prayer is recited at this point (after a brief introduction by the priest) in the Catholic Mass, with some varied English translation:

> Our Father, who art in heaven, hallowed be thy name. Thy kingdom come. Thy will be done, on Earth as it is in heaven. Give us this day our daily bread. And forgive us our trespasses, as we forgive those who trespass against us. Lead us not into temptation, but deliver us from evil.

The 1928 BCP adds:
> For thine is the kingdom, and the power, and the glory, for ever and ever. Amen.

After praying, the priest says, "Lord Jesus Christ, who said to your Apostles: Peace I leave you, my peace I give you; look not on our sins, but on the faith of your Church, and graciously grant her peace and unity in accordance with your will. Who live and reign for ever and ever".

*The Lord's prayer can be unpacked to seven or more components: 1) **invocation** ("our Father"), 2) **honor** to his holy name ("hallowed be thy name"), 3) **submission** ("thy will be done"), 4) **supplication** ("give us..."), 5) **reconciliation and forgiveness** ("forgive us..."), 6) **guidance** ("lead us...") and 7) **deliverance** ("deliver us..."). It was these components that Jesus taught were of utmost importance and what the catechism considers "truly the summary of the whole Gospel". NOTE: this is the author's own analysis. For other slightly varied interpretations a quick Internet search will provide others.*

The 1928 BCP addition is a protestant doxology that is not specifically part of the Catholic Mass. [18] Protestants who had converted to Catholicism in the U.S. over the years had been used to reciting it, and were explained they could silently recite it in prayer, but not aloud in public. [18] It is today, however, a fairly common practice.

Another practice fairly new, but also common in the U.S., is for the congregation to hold hands while reciting the Lord's prayer. This too is not part of the Mass, nor required. [18] The future of these practices are uncertain at best in that which is the ever-evolving Catholic Mass.

*"**The** sign of peace", "a sign of peace" or even "**some** sign of peace" varies as well, depending on the parish or culture, similarly to what "the" sign of peace" might be. [9] For instance, in Lithuania one would not see anyone shake hands in Mass, as in the U.S., much less hug or kiss; rather, a head-nod is given.*

Jesus responded, "Amen I say to you, whoever does not eat my body and does not drink my blood...has no life in them." [45]

Either the body or blood may be taken as Eucharist, not necessarily both. But taking both is said to be the fullness of the sacrament. [9]

The priest wishes the congregation peace: "The peace of the Lord be with you always." The deacon or, in his absence, the priest may then invite those present to offer each other the sign of peace. The form of the sign of peace varies: a handshake or a bow between strangers, or a kiss/hug between family members

The song "Lamb of God" is then sung while the priest breaks the bread and distributes communion to the lay ministers, who will then help distribute to the rest of the congregation.

Upon approaching the Eucharist, the recipient bows or nods. When administering Communion, the minister states to the recipient, "the body of Christ" or "the Blood of Christ". The recipient acknowledges this with "amen."

The recipient then returns to his or her pew to pray, most often kneeling, but sometimes sitting depending on health or age.

The sacred vessels are then purified by the priest and he recites another prayer.

CONCLUDING RITE

Announcements are then made casually, typically regarding parish events or coming Catholic feast days.

The priest then gives his blessing to the congregation and then concludes with some formal dialog between the priest and congregation ("the Lord be with you", etc.).

The deacon then dismisses the congregation, and the priest, the deacon and the altar boys or girls precess out of the church to music. Proper protocol is that the congregation sings the final hymn before leaving themselves, as the hymns are prayers in themselves.

There are several dismissals the deacon may use, such as "go forth..." or "the Mass has ended, go in peace..." [18]

CONCLUSION

Following and reading responses during Mass is important for those exploring Catholicism, but this booklet was drafted so as to try to explain the origins and practices of the Catholic mass as it remains today, as well as some of the Catholic beliefs that lead to these rites. The history of the Catholic Mass is rich and is always in flux, but with proper overview, it is

1 Corinthians 3: 10, "According to the Grace of God given to me, as a wise architect, I have laid the foundation and another builds upon it. But let everyone take care in how he builds from here." [46]

> *1 Corinthians 3: 11-15...*
>
> *"No one can build any foundation except that which is laid by Christ Jesus.*
>
> *"Now, if anyone builds upon this foundation, gold, silver, precious stones, wood, hay, stubble, then everyone's work shall be obvious; for the day of the Lord will declare it, because it shall be revealed in fire; and the fire shall challenge every man's work and show it for what it is.*
>
> *"If anyone's work stands after it is challenged, which he or she has built there upon, then he or she will receive reward.*
>
> *"If anyone's work burns, he or she will suffer that loss; be he or she themselves will still be saved, yet so as by fire."* [47]

something than anyone can learn and come to understand.

There are today, and have been for centuries, many misconceptions of how Catholics practice their faith. But one misconception that should perhaps be sought to overcome is anything that leads one to believe that the Catholic Mass has any other origins outside scripture, Jesus' teaching or the earliest of Christian practices. And today, wherever in the world one travels, from culture to culture or language to language, the one constancy that can be found in every Catholic parish are the rites as described herein, and the reasoning as explained.

REFERENCES

1. **Acts 19:17-18** Douay-Rheims 1899 American Edition (DRA), [18] And many of them that believed, came confessing and declaring their deeds.
2. **1 Timothy 6:12** Douay-Rheims 1899 American Edition (DRA), [12] Fight the good fight of faith: lay hold on eternal life, whereunto thou art called, and hast confessed a good confession before many witnesses.
3. **Acts 2:42** Douay-Rheims 1899 American Edition (DRA), [42] And they were persevering in the doctrine of the apostles, and in the communication of the breaking of bread, and in prayers.
4. **Eugene LaVerdiere** (1996), "The Eucharist in the New Testament and the Early Church".
5. **Vatican Council, & Catholic Church.** (1965). *Dogmatic constitution on divine revelation, November 18, 1965*. Washington, D.C: National Catholic Welfare Conference.
6. **Catholic Church., Donovan, J., & Catholic Church.** (1829). *The catechism of the Council of Trent: Published by command of Pope Pius the fifth*. New York: Catholic School Book Co.
7. **Leviticus 9:4-5** Douay-Rheims 1899 American Edition (DRA), [4] Also a bullock and a ram for peace offerings: and immolate them before the Lord, offering for the sacrifice of every one of them flour tempered with oil; for today the Lord will appear to you. [5] They brought therefore all things that Moses had commanded before the door of the tabernacle: where when all the multitude stood,
8. **Luke 22:19-20** Douay-Rheims 1899 American Edition (DRA), [19] And taking bread, he gave thanks, and brake; and gave to them, saying: This is my body, which is given for you. Do this for a commemoration of me. [20] In like manner the chalice also, after he had supped, saying: This is the chalice, the new testament in my blood, which shall be shed for you.
9. **Catechism of the Catholic Church**, 2nd ed. Washington, DC: United States Catholic Conference, 2000.
10. **Hebrews 10:11-14** Douay-Rheims 1899 American Edition (DRA), [11] And every priest indeed standeth daily ministering, and often offering the same sacrifices, which can never take away sins. [12] But this man offering one sacrifice for sins, for ever sitteth on the right hand of God, [13] From henceforth expecting, until his enemies be made his footstool. [14] For by one oblation he hath perfected for ever them that are sanctified.
11. **John 14:20** Douay-Rheims 1899 American Edition (DRA), [20] In that day you shall know, that I am in my Father, and you in me, and I in you.
12. **Benedict XVI**, Post-Synodal Apostolic Exhortation Sacramentum Caritatis.
13. **Mark 1:4** Douay-Rheims 1899 American Edition (DRA), [4] John was in the desert baptizing, and preaching the baptism of penance, unto remission of sins.

14. **Nehemiah 9:1-3** Douay-Rheims 1899 American Edition (DRA), And in the four and twentieth day of the month the children of Israel came together with fasting and with sackcloth, and earth upon them. [2] And the seed of the children of Israel separated themselves from every stranger: and they stood, and confessed their sins, and the iniquities of their fathers. [3] And they rose up to stand: and they read in the book of the law of the Lord their God, four times in the day, and four times they confessed, and adored the Lord their God.

15. **Andrew Chugg,** "*Alexander's Lovers*", 2006.

16. **Bowing,** https://en.wikipedia.org/wiki/Bowing.

17. **Maurice Hassett,** "*History of the Christian Altar*" in Catholic Encyclopedia 1907

18. **General Instruction of the Roman Missal,** 233.

19. **Ceremonial of Bishops,** 72

20. **1 Corinthians 10:15-17** Douay-Rheims 1899 American Edition (DRA), [15] I speak as to wise men: judge ye yourselves what I say. [16] The chalice of benediction, which we bless, is it not the communion of the blood of Christ? And the bread, which we break, is it not the partaking of the body of the Lord? [17] For we, being many, are one bread, one body, all that partake of one bread.

21. **1 Corinthians 11:26-27** Douay-Rheims 1899 American Edition (DRA), [26] For as often as you shall eat this bread, and drink the chalice, you shall shew the death of the Lord, until he come. [27] Therefore whosoever shall eat this bread, or drink the chalice of the Lord unworthily, shall be guilty of the body and of the blood of the Lord.

22. **Matthew 18:20** Douay-Rheims 1899 American Edition (DRA), [20] For where there are two or three gathered together in my name, there am I in the midst of them.

23. **Matthew 4:1-2** Douay-Rheims 1899 American Edition (DRA), Then Jesus was led by the spirit into the desert, to be tempted by the devil. [2] And when he had fasted forty days and forty nights, afterwards he was hungry.

24. **Mark 9:27-28** Douay-Rheims 1899 American Edition (DRA), [27] And when he was come into the house, his disciples secretly asked him: Why could not we cast him out? [28] And he said to them: This kind can go out by nothing, but by prayer and fasting.

25. **Acts 15:4-6** Douay-Rheims 1899 American Edition (DRA), [4] And when they were come to Jerusalem, they were received by the church, and by the apostles [bishops] and elders [priests], declaring how great things God had done with them. [5] But there arose some of the sect of the Pharisees that believed, saying: They must be circumcised, and be commanded to observe the law of Moses. [6] And the apostles [bishops] and elders [priests] assembled to consider of this matter.

26. **James 5:14** Douay-Rheims 1899 American Edition (DRA), [14] Is any man sick among you? Let him bring in the priests of the church, and let them pray over him, anointing him with oil in the name of the Lord.

27. **Luke 4:38** Douay-Rheims 1899 American Edition (DRA), [38] And Jesus rising up out of the synagogue, went into Simon's house. And Simon's wife's mother was taken with a great fever, and they besought him for her.

28. **1 Corinthians 7:8-9** Douay-Rheims 1899 American Edition (DRA), [8] But I say to the unmarried, and to the widows: It is good for them if they so continue, even as I. [9] But if they do not contain themselves, let them marry. For it is better to marry than to be burnt.
29. **1 Corinthians 7:32-34** Douay-Rheims 1899 American Edition (DRA), [32] But I would have you to be without solicitude. He that is without a wife, is solicitous for the things that belong to the Lord, how he may please God. [33] But he that is with a wife, is solicitous for the things of the world, how he may please his wife: and he is divided. [34] And the unmarried woman and the virgin thinketh on the things of the Lord, that she may be holy both in body and in spirit. But she that is married thinketh on the things of the world, how she may please her husband.
30. **Acts 6:1-5** Douay-Rheims 1899 American Edition (DRA), 6 And in those days, the number of the disciples increasing, there arose a murmuring of the Greeks against the Hebrews, for that their widows were neglected in the daily ministration. [2] Then the twelve calling together the multitude of the disciples, said: It is not reason that we should leave the word of God, and serve tables. [3] Wherefore, brethren, look ye out among you seven men of good reputation, full of the Holy Ghost and wisdom, whom we may appoint over this business. [4] But we will give ourselves continually to prayer, and to the ministry of the word. [5] And the saying was liked by all the multitude. And they chose Stephen, a man full of faith, and of the Holy Ghost, and Philip, and Prochorus, and Nicanor, and Timon, and Parmenas, and Nicolas, a proselyte of Antioch.
31. **2 Timothy 4:22** Douay-Rheims 1899 American Edition (DRA), [22] The Lord Jesus Christ be with thy spirit. Grace be with you. Amen.
32. **John 20:23** Douay-Rheims 1899 American Edition (DRA), [23] Whose sins you shall forgive, they are forgiven them; and whose sins you shall retain, they are retained.
33. **Matthew 17:19** Douay-Rheims 1899 American Edition (DRA), [19] Jesus said to them: Because of your unbelief. For, amen I say to you, if you have faith as a grain of mustard seed, you shall say to this mountain, Remove from hence hither, and it shall remove; and nothing shall be impossible to you.
34. **N. Lewis**, "Leitourgia and related terms," Greek, Roman and Byzantine Studies.
35. **John 1:14** Douay-Rheims 1899 American Edition (DRA), [14] And the Word was made flesh, and dwelt among us, (and we saw his glory, the glory as it were of the only begotten of the Father,) full of grace and truth.
36. **1 Corinthians 12:3** Douay-Rheims 1899 American Edition (DRA), [3] Wherefore I give you to understand, that no man, speaking by the Spirit of God, saith Anathema to Jesus. And no man can say the Lord Jesus, but by the Holy Ghost.
37. **Linda Woodhead**, "Christianity: a Very Short Introduction", 2004.
38. **Felix Just, S.J., Ph.D.,** *"Lectionary Statistics", http://catholic-resources.org/Lectionary/Statistics.htm* .
39. **First Council of Nicaea**, 325 AD.

40. **David Patton**, *"The World's Biggest Charity"*, http://www.catholicherald.co.uk/issues/february-17th-2017/a-worldwide-force-for-good/ .

41. **1 John 4:7** Douay-Rheims 1899 American Edition (DRA), [7] Dearly beloved, let us love one another, for charity is of God. And every one that loveth, is born of God, and knoweth God.

42. **Exodus 34:18** Douay-Rheims 1899 American Edition (DRA), [18] Thou shalt keep the feast of the unleavened bread. Seven days shalt thou eat unleavened bread, as I commanded thee in the time of the month of the new corn: for in the month of the springtime thou camest out from Egypt.

43. **John 6:59-61** Douay-Rheims 1899 American Edition (DRA), [59] This is the bread that came down from heaven. Not as your fathers did eat manna, and are dead. He that eateth this bread, shall live for ever. [60] These things he said, teaching in the synagogue, in Capharnaum. [61] Many therefore of his disciples, hearing it, said: This saying is hard, and who can hear it?

44. **Catholic Encyclopedia**, *"Epiclesis"*, Revised 2007.

45. **John 6:54** Douay-Rheims 1899 American Edition (DRA), [54] Then Jesus said to them: Amen, amen I say unto you: Except you eat the flesh of the Son of man, and drink his blood, you shall not have life in you.

46. **1 Corinthians 3:10** Douay-Rheims 1899 American Edition (DRA), [10] According to the grace of God that is given to me, as a wise architect, I have laid the foundation; and another buildeth thereon. But let every man take heed how he buildeth thereupon.

47. **1 Corinthians 3:11-15** Douay-Rheims 1899 American Edition (DRA), [11] For other foundation no man can lay, but that which is laid; which is Christ Jesus. [12] Now if any man build upon this foundation, gold, silver, precious stones, wood, hay, stubble: [13] Every man's work shall be manifest; for the day of the Lord shall declare it, because it shall be revealed in fire; and the fire shall try every man's work, of what sort it is. [14] If any man's work abide, which he hath built thereupon, he shall receive a reward. [15] If any man's work burn, he shall suffer loss; but he himself shall be saved, yet so as by fire.

48. **John 2:9-10** Douay-Rheims 1899 American Edition (DRA), [9] And when the chief steward had tasted the water made wine, and knew not whence it was, but the waiters knew who had drawn the water; the chief steward calleth the bridegroom, [10] And saith to him: Every man at first setteth forth good wine, and when men have well drunk, then that which is worse. But thou hast kept the good wine until now.

Additional copies of this booklet may be ordered at Amazon. Search using the keywords "catholic mass J N Cook" or simply look it up directly using the ISBN: 9781718073234.

If you have already purchased this booklet, *please leave a review at Amazon*. Because the audience of this booklet's individual faith is uniquely in communion (or coming into communion) with the Catholic faith, reviews are essential for those discerning purchase of this booklet, whether for themselves or their parish. This in turn helps strengthen and grow this ministry and the RCIA ministry on a whole.

If you would like to order larger quantities of this booklet, there are four "Kindle Countdown Deals" dates at Amazon for this title, scheduled four times per year, each run for four days. The Kindle Countdown Deals begin and end at noon and begin with the prices below. Note: this is an automated process.

Details:

Begin Date	Day 1	Day 2	Day 3	Day 4	Day 5
Jan 1st	$1	$2	$3	$4	End
April 1st	$1	$2	$3	$4	End
July 1st	$1	$2	$3	$4	End
Oct 1st	$1	$2	$3	$4	End

Printed in Great Britain
by Amazon